Called to SERVE

by Travis Hardin
The Young Writers Series

Called to Serve
Copyright © 2007 by The Benchmark Group LLC
ALL RIGHTS RESERVED

Published by:
The Benchmark Group LLC
148 Del Crest Drive Suite One
Nashville, TN 37217-4640
BenchmarkGroup1@aol.com

The integrity of the upright will guide them. Proverbs 11:3a

in association with:
McDougal Publishing
P.O. Box 3595
Hagerstown, MD 21742-3595
www.mcdougalpublishing.com

ISBN 978-1-58158-108-9

Printed in the United States of America
For Worldwide Distribution

Contents

Acknowledgements 5
Dedication 6
One: The Window 7
Two: Out of Breath 13
Three: Sunday Morning 19
Four: Once upon a Dawn 27
Five: Not the Same Anymore 31
Six: At Twilight 37
Seven: On the Trail 43
Eight: In the Dark 49
Nine: A Case of Mistaken Identity 55
Ten: A Soft Whisper 61
Eleven: Dazzling Skies 67
Twelve: Rain on the Rooftop 73
Thirteen: A Dying Eye 79
Fourteen: A Different World 85
Epilogue: Finding Closure 91

Acknowledgements

I would like to thank my English teacher for the past four years, Terry Klempner, for encouraging me (okay forcing me) to write and write and write. Without Mr. Klempner, this book would have never been written. Also, thanks to my parents for all of their support and encouragement.

Travis Hardin

This novel is dedicated to Ralph Curtis Shirley, my great-grandfather, whom I never got to meet, and my great-grandmother Myrtle Shirley Caudell. They exemplify a generation willing to give their all for our country and to go on when tragedy comes. Without them, I wouldn't be here.

Travis

CHAPTER ONE

The Window

A knock at the front door awoke the man who was sound asleep on the couch. He slowly got up and rubbed his eyes for a moment. Once again, somebody knocked on the door. This time the man hurried over to the door and opened it. He saw that it was his local mailman.

"Hey, Curt, how are you doing today?" the mailman said wiping his brow from delivering mail in the hot Georgia sun.

"I'm doing pretty well. How's your day going?" Ralph Curtis Shirley, or Curt for short, answered.

"I'm doing great. Here's your mail. See you later!" the mailman said.

"See you later," Ralph said tiredly. He closed the door behind him and walked back to the couch. He started sorting through the maze of letters until something caught his attention. An envelope with the seal of the U.S. Army was in front of him. Instantly, he sat up wide awake. He quickly tore open the envelope and ripped out the letter. His eyes quickly scanned down the paper. He couldn't believe what the letter said, so he read it again. Fear seized him and his hands started to shake.

Thoughts started to race across his mind. His greatest fear had finally caught up with him. He was going to war!

Curt had known this day was eventually going to come, even though he had been hoping for a miracle. Since the war had started, Curt had been lucky and had not been called up for active military duty. He was hoping that the end of the war would come soon. But since the D-day invasion, Curt had an ever-present feeling that his draft notice would come first. The Army needed men for the final push into the heart of Germany. He had always thought that having two kids might keep him out of the war, but his situation apparently hadn't been unique enough to make him exempt.

His problem became more difficult that night at dinner. Curt sat down at the table with his wife, Myrtle, and his two kids, Mary and Betty. His daughters were only babies and couldn't sense the turmoil he felt inside, but Myrtle did.

"What's wrong?" asked Myrtle.

"Well," replied Curt, "I have to show you something that came in the mail today." He reached into his pocket and pulled out his draft notice. She immediately saw who the letter was from and started to cry.

"No!" she cried, "They can't make you go!" He took her into his arms and let her cry into his shoulder.

"When are you leaving?" Myrtle asked.

Curt was silent for a few moments and then replied,

"I have to be at the train station on Tuesday morning. Five days from now." Curt and his wife sat in silence for the rest of the evening.

That weekend, Curt made it his goal to spend as much time as possible with his family. On Friday night, they scraped up enough money to go to Clayton and see a movie. It was supposed to be a comedy, but they weren't laughing. After the movie was over, they went outside and walked up and down the streets of Clayton.

"What do you want? Whatever you want, you can have it," Curt told Myrtle and the girls.

"Anything?" Myrtle repeated.

"Anything," he repeated. Myrtle took Curt's hand and led him down the street to the toy shop. She pointed to two twin dolls in the window.

"Is that what you really want?" Curt asked. Myrtle only nodded and looked at their baby girls. "Okay then. That's what they'll get," he said. Ten minutes later, both girls were clutching their dolls.

"And what do you want?" Curt said gently to his wife.

She hesitated for a moment and then whispered into his ear, "I want you to stay here with me."

"Don't worry. I'll be back home before you know it. Nothing can keep me from coming home," he answered with as much assurance as he could. This somewhat comforted her, and they enjoyed the rest of the evening. The family spent Saturday and Sunday relaxing with each other. On Sunday morning, Curt attended his last church service before he left. Curt and his wife spent a lot of time on Sunday night praying that everything would be okay.

Monday was a very long day for Curt. First, he had to pack up the things that he was allowed to take with him. He tried to keep it simple, but he ended up packing a lot of pictures. For some reason, as he looked around, everything about his home seemed especially dear to him today. The living room with its simple couch and chair were so comfortable. The house had just gotten electricity recently. He was going to miss this place so much when he left. But he would miss the people in the house much more. That night, while he was lying down to sleep for his last time there, he thought about what was going to happen in the next few months and maybe years. It was going to be tough, but he was confident that he would make it.

At six o' clock on Tuesday morning, Curt and his wife and the girls left the house and got in the car to go to the Clayton train station. They drove through the foothills that surrounded their farm, until they came to an overlook that looked down at the town of Clayton. Curt looked out of the window and silently said goodbye to his home. They entered the town, and pulled into the parking lot at the train station. As they all got out of the car, Mary and Betty yawned and rubbed their eyes. It was still pretty early for them to be getting up. Curt grabbed his bag and walked into the train yard.

He was amazed by how many men stood nearby waiting for the train. There must have been one hundred men. Suddenly, someone from behind him tapped him on the back.

"Hey, Curt. Haven't seen you in a while," he said.

Curt turned around and saw that it was Marcus Caudell. He and Curt had been good friends during high school.

"Marcus, what are you doing here?" Curt said.

"I'm guessing the same thing you are. I got a letter in the mail last week," Marcus said.

"I want you to meet my wife, Myrtle, and my girls, Betty and Mary." Curt said. They smiled and started talking to each other. A whistle disturbed the chatter and the train station became deathly quiet. A black train pulled slowly into the station and let out one final whistle.

A man stepped out of the train and yelled, "All aboard!"

Curt turned to his wife and kids and said, "I don't want you to worry about me. I'll be fine. Just pray for me and I'll be back before you know it." He embraced and kissed them all and walked towards the train. He hesitated and looked back one last time before boarding. He stepped aboard and found an available seat. He looked out of the window by his seat and saw his family.

For the first time in front of his family, a tear rolled down his face. This window was the only thing separating him from the most precious people in his life. He looked up again and waved goodbye for the last time to them. The train started to move, and as he passed them, he mouthed "I love you!" He put his head against the window and closed his eyes. It finally hit Curt that this could be the last time that he ever saw his family. That thought bothered him, so he put it out of his mind. He made a vow that he would come back to his family. Nothing would stop him. Nothing could.

CHAPTER TWO

Out of Breath

Curt's head suddenly slammed into the seat in front of him. He woke up and rubbed his aching head. All the men in the cab got up and started heading for the exit. Curt slowly figured out why they had stopped. After a full day riding on the train, they had finally arrived at Camp Polk, Louisiana. Marcus Caudell had it easy. All he had to do was ride the train to Atlanta. He had been sent to Fort Benning, Georgia. The lucky men on this train, however, had to ride all the way to Louisiana.

Curt grabbed his bag off the rack above him and got off the train. The heat and humidity just about knocked him down. The camp reminded him of a prison he had seen back home. High fences surrounded the entire complex and guards watched the gates. Curt followed the other men to a building where all the men were getting registered.

When Curt's turn came, a secretary asked him, "Sir, what is your name and state of origin?"

He answered, "Ralph Curtis Shirley and I am from Georgia." He continued to follow the line to where the men received their uniforms. He got his olive drab shorts and pants, a couple white t-shirts, and a pair of combat boots. Next, he went down the line to where the men were getting haircuts. He ran his hand through his hair and jokingly said goodbye to it. He sat down in a chair where a barber proceeded to shave off most of Curt's hair. They didn't take the time to be gentle. After he got the haircut and was rubbing his sore scalp, another man assigned him to a barrack. They assigned him to Barrack C, which was the third barrack in a line that stretched across an entire field.

Curt entered into the barrack, and quickly grabbed one of the few remaining bunks. He started to organize his living area, when the man on the top bunk looked down at Curt.

"Hey, man what's your name?" he said with an obvious country accent.

"My name's Curt Shirley. I'm from Georgia. What about you?" Curt answered back.

"My name is Joe Lovell. I'm from Mississippi. Nice to meet you," Joe answered.

The rest of the day was spent filling out paperwork and getting his instructions for the next day. That night all the men of Barrack C got together and introduced themselves to each other. There was Jim Covett from North Carolina, Andy Collins from West Virginia, Steve Davis from Nebraska, and Dave Richards from New York. They all seemed to be really nice guys, and everyone got to know each other pretty well that first night.

They all felt better about being at boot camp... until early the next morning.

At five o' clock the next morning, a bugle interrupted the silence. All the men in the barracks awoke abruptly, some of them jumping up like they'd been shot.

The lights were suddenly switched on, and a giant of a man screamed, "Get out of your stinking beds, you maggots!" Immediately, everyone stood up and got dressed as quickly as they could. Then the man decided to introduce himself, "My name is Sergeant Jackson. I will be the man who makes your life miserable for the next two months. Now get outside on the lawn!"

Everyone scrambled outside and lined up single file. The first activity for the day was the obstacle course. It was a pathetic sight to see all those grown men embarrass themselves on the obstacle course. But, as the morning wore on, the men gradually got better.

The sergeants then told them their schedules for the next few months. Exercise lasted from five to eight in the morning. Breakfast was from eight to nine. Then from nine to twelve they would be involved in military tactics and training. Twelve to one was lunch. One to six was more military tactics and training. Six to seven was dinner. The rest of the night was for rest. Curt didn't exactly love the exercise in the morning, and the military tactics were difficult to learn.

The first two weeks of boot camp were very difficult

and consisted mostly of physical training. The third week was when the fun started, or at least the fun for Curt. One morning during the third week, they drove the recruits out to a shooting range. Curt secretly loved this part of training. Back in Georgia, Curt had always loved going hunting on his free days. It was something that he used to do with his dad.

The sergeants first handed each man a M1 Garand. This gun was a semi-automatic rife that fired thirty caliber rounds. Each recruit went up to the firing line and aimed at a target about fifty yards away. One of the sergeants signaled for the men to fire. Shot after shot rang out until every man's gun was empty. Then each target was checked for accuracy. Most of the men had either missed the target completely or landed only one or two shots. Curt, however, had hit the target with every one of his eight bullets. The men who didn't do so well were then taught how to shoot.

Throughout the next few weeks, the men were introduced to an array of weapons. They trained on how to use the Thompson sub-machine gun, the BAR machine gun, the 45 Colt pistol, and the M1 Carbine. Some men learned specialties in other kinds of guns. Since Curt had experience with guns before and was a good marksman, he was assigned a Springfield sniper rifle. Other men, who were not as lucky, operated flamethrowers, 30 caliber machine guns, and 50 caliber machine guns.

The men were starting to look more like soldiers and were becoming a close-knit group. They learned combat maneuvers and how to drive military vehicles. About two weeks before Curt graduated, he found out what division he would be in. Sergeant Jones told the men that they would be in the 89th Cavalry Recon Squadron, which was a part of the 9th Armored Division.

After that meeting, the training started to get really difficult. The second to last week, the exercise sessions were lengthened. Every night, Curt went to bed totally exhausted, and he could tell that everyone else was too. He really wished that he was home in his own bed. The only consolation was reading and rereading the letters from Myrtle and smiling at the pictures Mary and Betty had drawn for him. He particularly liked the one where Mary had drawn him looking like a giant stork with black hair. He tried not to tear up when he read Myrtle's words:

Dear Curt,
The girls and I miss you so much. We are doing fine, so don't go worrying about us. You just take care of yourself and make sure you come back home to us soon. I don't think I'll ever get used to being alone here without you. You are my life, and I love you so much! I see Momma and Daddy a lot, and my brothers and sisters are keeping me company. I got your last letter. Those Army boys are

> sure lucky to get such a good shot as you. I know you'll
> be a big help to the Allies when you get over there. Well, I
> better go and get the girls' supper ready. Remember how
> much we love you.
>
> Love,
Myrtle

Graduation day finally came, and everyone was overjoyed. There was a small ceremony where the sergeants shook the hands of the recruits and gave them their new Army uniforms.

The hard part was about to begin.

The war in Europe had finally, after three years, started to go in the Allies' favor. After the invasion of Normandy in June (1944), the Allies had slowly fought their way through France. The final strike into Germany was going to be tough. Curt's squadron's first order was to travel to New Orleans to get to the troop ship. Once again, all of the men of the 89th Cavalry boarded the trains and left Camp Polk. A couple of hours later, the men arrived in New Orleans. The next day the men of the 89th Cavalry would board the Queen Mary, travel to France, and eventually to the battlefields of Germany.

CHAPTER THREE

Sunday Morning

That Sunday morning was a hot one in New Orleans. The men of the 89th Cavalry awoke to a day that some had looked forward to and some had dreaded. When the men got on the Queen Mary, they would finally be going into action. What most of them did not know was that there was a pretty good chance that none of them would even make it to Europe. German U-boats still patrolled the Atlantic like roving wolves. Even if they did get to France, many of them would not make it back to their homes in America.

Curt and the rest of his division arrived at the dock about 8:00 a.m. The rest of the 9th Armored Division had arrived earlier in the morning. The Queen Mary was a giant ship. The soldiers were housed in the first few floors of the ship. The hull had been cleared out so that equipment could be stored below. The crew was in the process of loading tanks, jeeps, artillery, guns, and ammunition. After an hour, it was finally Curt's turn to get on board. He walked up the gangplank and greeted a tall sailor.

"What division are you in?" the sailor asked.

"89th Cavalry," Curt replied.

"Your quarters are below deck. Have a good voyage," he said.

"Thanks," Curt replied. He walked below deck and saw a familiar face. There was Joe Lovell with a silly grin on his face.

"Hey, Curt. Are you ready to go kill some *krauts*?" Joe said.

"I wouldn't worry about that too much until we get to France," Curt replied. "The way you shoot, I doubt that you'll be hitting anything anyways."

"That's pretty funny," Joe replied sarcastically.

"Are you not scared at all?" Curt asked. Joe's expression got a little more serious.

"Sometimes, I get a little scared about what's going to happen over there." He replied.

"To tell you the truth, Joe, I'm scared stiff. Whenever I think about this war, I feel nauseated. The fighting itself doesn't bother me, its being away from home for so long. I don't think I can do it," Curt said.

A fog horn sounded suddenly and a voice came over the intercom saying, "The voyage is about to get under way. Report to your barracks."

Joe and Curt found their barracks on the second floor. It certainly didn't look like a luxury ship. Bunk beds covered the room and about fifty people were crowded into the room. Curt could already tell that he was not going to enjoy this trip. Suddenly, Curt felt himself sliding backwards. The ship had finally left the dock.

Time goes by very slowly when a person is bored. The first day of the trip seemed like an eternity. The ship was going at a steady pace of 4 knots. At that speed, the trip would take about a week, maybe a little more. At night, the sea looked a lot different than it did in the day.

One night, Joe commented, "I never knew such huge darkness existed, did you?"

"It sure is different from the beautiful mountains back home," Curt answered. Sleeping was very difficult the first night. The ship kept rocking back and forth, which made it almost impossible to get comfortable.

The soldiers on board tried desperately to deal with boredom. Card games and telling stories were the most popular events on board, besides eating of course. On the morning of the third day, two smaller ships appeared beside the ship. Curt later found out that they were Destroyers. Their job was to protect the Queen Mary from submarine threats. Once again the nagging feeling came back, and Curt was actually afraid that he might die.

That night, Curt's fears were almost realized. At dusk, Curt and Joe were sitting on the deck when an alarm went off.

"All hands on deck. This is not a drill. Battle stations!" the voice on the intercom yelled. Curt looked off at the Destroyer to his right and saw them rolling barrels off the back. For a few moments he wondered what they were doing, but then an explosion erupted out of the water. The Destroyers were dropping depth charges. That could only mean one thing. A U-boat!

Explosion after explosion echoed through the night. Suddenly a sailor yelled out, "Torpedo!" Everyone looked over the side and sure enough there was a white trail coming through the water. Time stood still as the torpedo approached the hull. The Queen Mary accelerated to try to outrun the torpedo. The torpedo passed by the back of the ship, missing it by about ten feet. Everyone breathed a quick sigh of relief. A few more depth charges went off and this time one explosion sounded different. Instead of showering water into the air, fire and oil spewed out of the water, the telltale sign of a direct hit. After a minute or two, oil came floating to the surface. The men all shouted and celebrated for a moment. Then amazingly, the crew of all three ships simply went back to work. Curt gasped at how close he had just come to dying.

For the rest of the trip, the soldiers tried to stay below deck. The fourth, fifth, and sixth days went by even more slowly. Curt tried to pass the time by writing a letter home. The rest of the time he spent just hanging out with the rest of the guys. In one letter, Curt wrote:

Dear Myrtle,
I pray that you and the girls are doing okay. I can't

believe how much I miss ya'll. I can't tell you where we are going. The censors would just black it out or cut it out anyway, but I am on my way. I will do my best to be a good soldier and conduct myself honorably, and most of all, to come back home to my precious family safe and soon! You be sure to ask for help from my family or yours if you need anything. I pray every night that God will look after you and the girls. I bet they're growing like weeds. I wish I could see them right now. I love your letters and the pictures the girls color for me. I don't know how the mail will run once I get to where I'm going, but I'll keep writing and you do the same. No matter what, remember I love you!

Your loving husband,
Curt

On the morning of the seventh day at sea, the captain came on the horn and told everyone that they would be at Normandy by that afternoon. Curt and his friends started to get jumpy. Once again, Joe and the others started to rant about the battles to come.

"The *krauts* don't have any idea what's coming their way," Joe started.

"Put a sock in it, Joe. We all know that you won't be shooting anything over here." Andy teased. Joe threw his pillow at Andy.

There wasn't going to be any combat that day, but they would be relieved to finally be off the ship. All day

Curt waited on the deck and strained to see the shore. At about 3 o'clock in the afternoon, Curt finally spotted a beach. As they got closer, they saw vehicles, ships, and people everywhere. Just a few months before, Germans had held this beach against the Allies.

The Queen Mary finally slowed down and stopped a few hundred yards off the beach. She could go no further without a tug helping her come in. The German machine gun nests still stood where they had been on D-day. A tug pulled the ship until the front of it was on dry land. From his view on the bow, Curt could see men unloading countless tanks, jeeps, and crates of ammunition off the ship. Then the sailors threw down the gangplank and the soldiers started to get off. One by one, the 9th Armored Division packed up their things and left the ship. At 5 o'clock, it was finally Curt's turn to leave the ship. As he took his first steps onto the sand, he finally understood what the sailors meant by sea legs.

All the soldiers were directed toward a group of tents where they were to be given their orders. They were also being issued equipment. The first man at a table asked, "What is your division?"

"9th Armored, 89th Cavalry Recon Squadron," Curt answered. The man searched through a stack of papers and handed one to Curt. At the top of the paper it said "Shirley, Ralph Curtis, 89th Cavalry Recon Squadron." He continued walking down the line and went to the area to pick up his equipment. Curt handed the second man his sheet of paper, and the man went back into a bunker. He came out with three items: a combat helmet with Curt's name inside, a Springfield rifle, and a box of ammunition. The man handed Curt his paper and went on to the next soldier.

Sergeant Jackson stood outside the tent and said, "89th Cavalry, meet up with me." Curt walked up and joined the group. The huge sergeant said, "Okay, I'm going to keep this short. Get some sleep tonight. We're going to be leaving at 7 o'clock tomorrow morning. This is the real thing."

They were heading to the front lines.

Curt saw Joe walking by lugging all his gear and called out, "Joe, wait up!" Joe turned with that wide grin of his and asked Curt, "You ready to go show them how it's done?"

"I don't know about that, but I'm gonna try to stay alive for as long as possible," Curt replied.

They both trudged on to their sleeping areas thinking about what was to come.

CHAPTER FOUR

Once upon a Dawn

Dawn came softly on that cool October day. Curt woke up to the sun rising softly over the Atlantic. Although the sun was not even overhead yet, already the beach was bustling with activity, the air filled with the sound of engines. Jeeps and tanks were set out in a line on the sand. The whole 9th Armored Division was preparing to leave. Curt went to an assigned jeep near the front of the line. He found out that the 89th Cavalry Recon Squadron would be leading the way into France. Curt would be driving, Joe was in the side seat, and Andy Collins was on the 50 caliber. All three men put their equipment in the back and got in their seats. Everyone got comfortable and waited for the convoy to move. Curt felt a sense of nervousness, but also excitement about going into battle.

A bugle sounded up ahead and the first jeep started to move. "Let's get ready to go!" Andy yelled. Curt stomped on the gas and the convoy started to leave the beach. They went up a sandy slope until they arrived in the French countryside. The area that used to be a beautiful place to live was now a horrible sight. Burned-out vehicles from both Allied and German forces littered the sides of the roads. Almost every field was littered with dead livestock. On the first day, the group saw countless fields that had been converted to graveyards. The first stop that day was in Carentan. That city had been home to bitter fighting just a month earlier. Some streets still had dead bodies lying in them. Curt felt nauseated as he passed by them. The 9th Armored stayed in Carentan that night but left early in the morning.

The second day in France held a lot more action than the first. As they were driving down the road, a shell exploded beside the front jeep. All of them swerved off the road and looked for enemies. Sergeant Jackson stood up and yelled, "Keep going, soldiers. It's just scattered mortar fire!" They continued down the roads, watching for more mortar fire. Nothing else happened that day or even the next day. About four days into the drive to the front lines, the 89th Cavalry got their first orders. They were to go ahead of the rest of the Division and scout for enemy troop movement.

The next morning, Curt's jeep and three others departed for a little town named St. Cherie. The First Infantry Division was waiting outside the town and getting ready for the push into Belgium. The jeeps stopped on a hilltop to scout the area around the town. A few of the men used binoculars while Curt looked through his Springfield scope at the town. All was quiet for about ten minutes, and then Curt spotted movement. He saw two men walking on the edge of the town. He looked closer and saw that they were Germans. Curt motioned for the rest of the men to look for more Germans. Suddenly a tank came in sight near the town.

"It's a Tiger," a sergeant said.

"What do we do?" Joe asked.

"We're going to take it out," he replied with a grin. The sergeant got on the radio and started talking. A few moments later, the booming of artillery sounded. Curt was still looking through his scope at the Germans. More Germans were coming through the town now. Five tanks and a few halftracks had also joined the infantry. The ground exploded around the Germans, and Curt watched in amazement at the power of the artillery. The tanks tried to escape, but each one was hit by American artillery. They were engulfed in flames, and the ammunition inside them detonated causing more carnage. The Germans tried to fall back into the safety of the town, but most were brought down by the shells. American Sherman tanks rolled out of the forest. Only a few of the Germans made it back inside the town. The recon group then headed down the hill themselves.

Joe was in the side seat carrying a BAR, and Andy was on the 50 caliber. Black columns of smoke rose over the town. Curt's jeep came into the town first and was immediately hit by fire. Bullets pinged off the hood, and Curt panicked. Andy opened up with the 50 and blew apart the windows where the bullets were coming from. Curt and Joe jumped out of the jeep and ran for cover.

Curt and Joe looked down the street for enemies.

Two Germans appeared out of a doorway and started running the other way. Before Curt even got a chance to shoot, Andy mowed them down with the 50 caliber. Curt was amazed at the carnage that that gun delivered. The 9th Armored tanks started to enter the town along with the rest of the 89th. A hissing sound followed by a stream of smoke traveled by Curt. A rocket hit the first tank in the turret, and it erupted in flames. Curt looked around the corner and brought his rifle to his shoulder. A hundred yards down the street, a long tube stuck out from an alley. The tube started to move and a man brought it to his shoulder. Curt quickly took aim and squeezed the trigger. The tube of the "Panzerschrek" rocket launcher rolled off of the German's shoulder, and the man slumped to the ground.

"Nice shot, Curt!" Joe yelled.

Suddenly, Curt noticed that he was still holding his breath, and he started to breathe again. The tanks rolled on ahead past Curt, Joe, and Andy and continued down the street. Curt felt a strange sense of guilt and pride at the same time. He had saved the tanks in his group, but he had also killed a human being for the first time. As they got back in their jeep, all three of the men were quiet. They didn't exactly know how to deal with their first combat experience. Curt couldn't look away as he passed the German he had shot just moments before. The man was lying face up in a pool of his own blood. It was the worst experience of Curt's life... up to that point.

CHAPTER FIVE

Not the Same Anymore

It took a full day for the 9th Armored to clear out the town of St. Cherie. They had only a few wounded, but three of their men had died. The German with the "Panzerschrek" killed them while they were in the tank. Curt didn't know how to respond to what had happened that day. He had learned that it was kill or be killed. That night, some of the men were celebrating taking the town, but Curt just sat back and watched. He had to prepare himself for what was going to come.

Over the next few weeks, the division made their way farther and farther west into France. They faced sporadic resistance, and only sustained a few injuries to their men. Curt was amazed at how few bodies he had to see before it didn't bother him anymore. As the weeks progressed, the temperature went down. By the beginning of November, it was about 40 degrees each day. The men were starting to get angry because they had no cold weather equipment. Headquarters kept telling them that the equipment was coming, but it didn't come.

In the month of November, it was very quiet, too quiet. The Germans retreated back into Belgium and eventually Germany. They left before a shot was fired. It was good that they were retreating, but it was puzzling. The Germans had never given up this quickly before. When the 9th Armored arrived in Belgium, they were told that they were to patrol the border and look for German activity. This was an assignment that was perfect for the 89th Recon. If they spotted anything that looked suspicious, they were to immediately call headquarters. At the moment, most divisions were driving west as fast as they could. Some of them had almost gotten to the Rhine River. One night the men started talking around the fire.

"Why are the Nazi's retreating like this?" Andy asked.

"Heck, I don't care as long as they keep going back," Curt responded.

"Sometimes it just bothers me that they're giving up so easily. I feel like it's a trap," he said. Truth be told, Curt was feeling exactly the same.

The job of patrolling the Belgian border was a toilsome task. At nights it would get so cold that the tanks' tracks would freeze up. Everyone soon learned that the tanks and jeeps could not stop moving long. Every once in a while, a small group of Germans would appear out of the thick Ardennes forest and fire a few shots at the Americans. Usually the tanks would fire at the Germans, and they would hurry back into the forest.

At dusk on December 1st the Germans struck with a different style of attack. Curt and his friends had just made a fire, and the camp was settling down for the night. They were all chatting when they heard distant booms. Immediately, everyone ran for cover, and the tanks were moved into the trees. A massive artillery attack came down on the clearing that they had just been in. Curt was deafened by the explosion of the shells. Almost as suddenly as the attack had started, the artillery stopped. The forest was quiet, and Curt had his rifle at the ready. For a few minutes, everyone remained motionless. Finally, the officers decided that it was all clear. Everyone slowly emerged out of the woods and walked to where they had set up camp. Deep craters marked what had been the camp site.

Curt hated artillery strikes just like everyone else. There was never any warning, and the destructive power was devastating. The Germans had mastered this technique over the last five years. The men in the 9th Armored Division were still "green." They had faced little combat and were not used to fighting day after day. Some of the men were ready to have a big fight with the Germans; Curt just wanted to go home.

The next day Curt found out their destination. They were going to Bastogne to meet up with the 101st Airborne in the town. Then they would be moving on to Germany. The first two weeks of December were bitterly cold. The group moved over 100 miles in those weeks. At night all the equipment would freeze up, and everyone tried to thaw themselves out by the fire. The poor men's winter clothes had not arrived yet. Strangely, the Germans never made another attack on the way to Bastogne. It almost felt too quiet making their way through the Ardennes forest. They knew the Germans were somewhere out there, but they had no idea where. On December 15, they finally made it to Bastogne. The 101st Airborne had arrived there just the day before.

Bastogne was a town that had been pretty devastated by war. It once had been a very beautiful alpine town, full of life and activity. It had become a deserted and bombed-out pile of rubble. Almost every building had been hit with artillery shells and bullets. Curt found an abandoned hotel on the main street and moved into a room on the ground floor for the night. It was the first time he had stayed indoors in over two months. The 101st guys were nice enough to treat the 9th Armored to a meal that night. There was a lot of laughing and talking with the airborne guys. Everybody had a good time, and most of them didn't get much sleep. And, as often happens, a few men had too much to drink that night.

At around midnight, Curt made his way toward his room. He was walking down the street, when he heard a very low rumbling sound. He listened for a moment more and then shrugged it off. He hobbled into bed and immediately fell into a deep sleep.

At 5 a.m. Curt awoke with a start. The rumbling had gotten louder. Curt ran to his window. He looked outside and saw men gathering. He quickly ran outside with his rifle.

"What's going on?" Curt asked Joe.

"I don't know, but we have been ordered to go find out!" Joe responded.

Curt sighed and headed for his jeep. Andy was already on the 50 caliber machine gun. Joe hopped in the front seat, and Curt got in the driver's side. Curt's jeep led a convoy of three jeeps and one tank out of the town. They followed a small road through the forest until they got to a wide clearing. They stopped the vehicles and hunkered down in the woods. The humming got louder and louder in the woods on the other side of the field. Suddenly, Curt saw movement through the trees. One tank appeared, then another, then another, until five tanks moved into the open field.

"Get on the radio…" Curt yelled.

"And, tell them what!" Joe yelled back. More tanks and infantry were moving into the field now.

"That we are under a major German attack!" Curt yelled.

CHAPTER SIX

At Twilight

The Germans were just a few hundred yards away from the group of jeeps now. A whole German division of tanks and half-tracks were coming across the field to take Bastogne. Only Curt's jeep and two others were in their way.

"Let's get out of here, NOW!" Joe yelled. All three jeep engines roared to life. Curt stomped on the gas and sped out of the woods. The two other jeeps followed closely. The nearest tanks and half-tracks erupted with gunfire. Shells hit in front of Curt's jeep and machine gun bullets tore through the trees beside them. The town was just coming into view, when the jeep in the rear got hit by a tank shell. It erupted in flames and slammed into a tree. Suddenly, a group of American tanks came into view and started to fire back. The German's tank fire stopped for a moment, giving Curt a chance to get into the town.

When they got back into the town, the rest of the 9th Armored Division was mounting up in their tanks and getting ready for a fight. A group of ten Sherman tanks left the town and went to engage the German forces. In a few moments, tank fire was heard, and the sounds of continuous explosions were heard for about five minutes. Suddenly, the firing stopped and there was only silence. Then something appeared at the town's entrance. The tanks in the town were about to fire, when they recognized the tanks as American. Only two of the ten tanks had returned. One wounded man climbed out of one of the tanks and hobbled over to the commanding officer.

"We only got one tank," he stuttered.

"Where are the rest of the tanks?" the officer asked.

"After we had lost eight of ours, they just retreated. They could've killed us all..." the tanker replied.

The officer stood there for a moment thinking, but then he stood up and said, "Listen up everyone. The Germans were just testing us. The real counterattack is going to come later." The officer then split the men into four groups. The 89th Cavalry was to defend the northern edge of the town. Parts of the 101st Airborne were going to be joining them.

At twilight, the 89th Cavalry left the town and entered the forest. They went a mile or two into the woods and spread out. Curt was told to dig a three foot deep foxhole. Andy dug a foxhole about twenty feet to his left and Joe was to his right. The rest of Curt's friends from basic training were scattered about. While he was digging, all Curt could think about was his family and how they were doing at home. He had been writing letters constantly, but the postal system wasn't the best in the European war front. He wanted to reassure them that he was going to be okay.

"It's about time the Germans started to give us a fight," Joe said.

"Just wait till the Germans show up in the morning. I don't think you will be grinning any more," Andy growled.

"What's his deal?" Joe asked.

"He's just afraid of what is about to come. They could be out there right now." Curt responded.

As the sun started to peak over the horizon, Curt suddenly realized how cold he was. The winter uniforms had still not come in, and no one had gloves or jackets. He sat down in his foxhole, and looked out into the forest. The Germans were out there somewhere watching and waiting. They could be watching him right then for all he knew. As he sat there waiting, it started to snow. For a few seconds, Curt forgot how cold he was as he watched the snow gently falling through the trees in the moonlight.

A few moments later, Curt forgot about both the snow and the cold. Dull explosions echoed through the woods. "Get down. We're getting shelled!" shouted Andy. Curt slouched down in his foxhole as the first shells started to hit. Snow and dirt flew high into the air as the shells hit the ground. Some shells hit the trees, and the trees blew in half. After the first couple of shells, all Curt could hear was a constant ringing with a few loud thumps when the shells hit. He looked over at Joe who was screaming in fear. Curt looked down at the shaking ground and said a quick prayer for safety. A few moments later, the shelling slowed and then came to a stop.

Everyone slowly got up and looked around. One man actually stepped out of his foxhole and started to walk down the line of foxholes. "Is everyone okay? Is anyone missing....," he asked. Suddenly the man went down with a shot to the chest. A loud yell rose up in the woods, and Curt looked to the north. Germans in white camouflage had suddenly started charging. The line started to return fire immediately. Curt picked up his rifle and took aim. He looked through the scope and lined the crosshairs on the nearest German. He squeezed the trigger, and the closest German went down in a heap. Joe and Andy opened up on the Germans next. The group of Germans stopped and tried to find cover for themselves. Joe stood up so he could take a clearer shot and then stumbled backwards and fell to the ground. Curt looked over at Joe clutching his chest.

"I'm hit!" he grunted.

"Joe, are you okay?" Curt yelled. Joe just looked at him but couldn't respond. Curt ran to Joe's foxhole. He had been shot in the chest and was losing blood fast.

"MEDIC!" Curt screamed. "You're going to be all right. Hang on, Joe. Where is that medic?" Curt yelled.

Joe looked into Curt's face for a few moments, and then his gaze went off into the woods. His gaze never left the woods. Joe died without saying a word. Curt sat there stunned. It seemed like nothing else was happening around him. He looked down at Joe, the man who had been his best friend since boot camp, and tears rolled down his face. Then anger welled up inside of Curt. He was filled with rage as he turned back to the Germans. He picked up Joe's automatic rifle and stood up to face the Germans. Curt let out a horrible yell and pulled the trigger. The nearest German tried to run but was cut down by the machine gun. Suddenly all of the Germans got out of their hiding places and started to retreat. Curt got out of the foxhole and sprinted after them. While he was yelling, he started shooting from the hip. Two of the Germans hit the ground. Curt was holding down the trigger, and the BAR ran out of ammo. Curt threw the gun to the ground, and pulled out his Colt 45. One German soldier tried to get up, but Curt shot him with the Colt. As the Germans tried to escape, Curt peeled off shot after shot with his pistol. Curt was about to pursue the Germans, but a hand pulled him back.

"It's over now, Curt," Andy said. Slowly, Curt's anger subsided. He became more aware of what was happening. He felt something wet and sticky all over him. He looked down at his hands and saw blood covering his uniform and hands. For a second, he thought he had been wounded, but then he realized whose blood it was. Curt looked over at Joe's foxhole and saw Joe lying there very peacefully. He then looked over at the German soldiers' bodies. Most of the Germans who had attacked them were lying on the ground in front of Curt.

Curt knew that their attacks had only begun. This wasn't the last time that they would see the Germans. The rest of the day, Curt helped move the American and German bodies, and then dug in for the night. The next day would only bring more death.

CHAPTER SEVEN

On the Trail

Christmas was very cold in Bastogne. The snow was getting deeper and deeper every day. The cold weather gear was scheduled, so they had been told, to arrive the next week. A few of the guys had gotten hypothermia or frost bite. At night, Curt sat near the campfire just to stay alive.

"Is anyone else cold here?" Andy asked.

"No, my hands are usually this shade of blue." Sergeant Jackson said sarcastically. Everyone started laughing at that comment.

"Yeah, by the way when are the uniforms going to come in?" Curt asked.

"Whenever command thinks it's time to send them," Jackson answered.

Every once in a while the Germans would send in an artillery strike that made Curt's life miserable. So far, the 101st and 9th Armored had held off every German advance. There were a lot of casualties. A few of Curt's friends had died over the last few weeks. But Joe's death had bothered him the most.

In the last week, American planes had been coming over on bombing runs. The day before, Curt had gone through the forest to see if the planes had been hitting their targets. He came to the edge of a field filled with burned-out tanks and half-tracks. German bodies littered the ground. A few weeks ago, this kind of destruction and bloodshed would have bothered him. Curt had finally realized that the Germans were his enemy. He was there to defeat them—until they killed him, he went home, or the war ended.

On December 26, Curt found out his next orders. The next day, the 101st was going to make a push and take the town of Foy. Curt's orders were to join a few men from the 89th and do reconnaissance in the area. Sgt. Jackson was going to take Curt, Andy, and two other men to do the job. Foy was about two miles away to the north. The 101st Airborne was waiting in the forest by the town to attack.

Early the morning of the 27th Sgt. Jackson led the group of men deep into the forest. As the sun started to rise above the horizon, the town of Foy came into view. The town appeared almost completely white... except for the German tanks and artillery.

Sgt. Jackson looked at Curt and said, "Get in the wood line on the west side of town, and then use a radio to tell us how many tanks and 88's there are." He put a radio on Curt's back. Curt grabbed his Springfield. He constantly kept his eyes on Foy as he crept through the tree line. German tanks and infantry owned this town. White German uniforms stood out against the stark black of the tanks and buildings.

Curt found a close cluster of trees about a hundred yards from the town. He crept into the trees and sat down in the darkness. Peering through the scope, he started his recon. He looked up and down the town and started counting troops, armor, and artillery. He estimated that there were at least five hundred Germans defending the town. He also counted two Tiger tanks, two Panzer tanks, five half-tracks, and five 88 millimeter cannons. Obviously, the city was armed to the teeth.

Since the Germans counterattacked on December 16, they had been trying to give up as little land as possible. If Foy fell to the Americans, the counterattack would be a failure. Curt got on the radio to Sgt. Jackson and relayed the information about the German strength. Sgt. Jackson told Curt to stay put for a few minutes and that they were going to come to find him. Curt relaxed and started to watch the town again. After a few minutes, Curt heard voices approaching from the woods. The Germans did too. The closest 88 millimeter cannon turned towards Curt's direction. Curt quickly looked down the scope at the cannon. The voices approaching were definitely American. The Germans on the cannon were getting ready to fire. Curt had to make a decision.

The silence was broken with a loud crack. The German officer directing the cannon slowly toppled to the ground. Curt quickly pulled the bolt back and pushed another bullet into the chamber. The German cannon fired a shot into the forest. A tree ten feet behind Curt blew in half. Curt quickly shot two more shots at the cannon. One more man fell off the cannon. The other two men quickly ran for cover. The other 88's had turned in Curt's direction. Curt heard four corresponding booms as shells exploded all around him. One explosion threw him into a tree behind him. The woods in front of him slowly faded into darkness

Curt awoke and was looking into the blue sky. Andy's face suddenly appeared over him.

"Wow, Curt, you took a pretty big hit there." Andy said.

"Am I alive?" Curt asked in a daze.

"Barely, I'm surprised that you didn't knock over that tree that you hit," Andy said. Curt felt the back of his head and felt a good bit of blood on his hand.

"Good grief, my head hurts," he sighed.

"The good news is that you woke up just in time for the show," Andy said laughing.

Curt slowly got up and looked out towards Foy. In the woods towards Curt's right a loud yell rose up as men from the 101st rushed out into the clearing beside the town. Mortars and artillery came down right on top of them. A lot of the men didn't even make it to the town itself. The men who did were under a lot of fire. The tanks were starting to move up to attack the

Americans, when the tanks from the 9th Armored Division entered the clearing. The American tanks were the first to fire. Shells completely obliterated the first German tanks. All that was left were smoldering piles of metal. Curt watched as the 101st went from house to house clearing them of Germans. After the 101st disabled all of the 88's, the Germans finally surrendered.

The 9th Armored was given the all clear to come into town. As Curt walked into town, death surrounded him. Americans and Germans lay side by side, most of them dead. The 101st took over two hundred men prisoner in Foy. All of the Americans were celebrating, while the Germans hung their heads in shame. A single shot broke the peace. Everyone dove for cover while the German sniper picked off helpless Americans. As soon as his position was located, a barrage of fire covered the building. All of the tanks fired into the building along with infantry rifles. The whole front of the building collapsed under the gun fire. Needless to say, there was no more German fire.

On this day the tide had turned against the Germans. Their oppressive counterattack had been turned into a full retreat. Curt knew at that point that Germany was taking in its dying breath. The problem was that it looked like Germany would fight harder for that last breath than they would for any before.

CHAPTER EIGHT
In the Dark

The Germans were now in retreat. Fifty more miles, and the Americans and British would be at the Rhine River. The winter clothes had finally arrived along with the mail that had been delayed for about three months. Curt quickly threw on the boots and gloves that had been given to him. His hands and face had been numb since Christmas. Nobody complained about the cold; all they had to do to be thankful was to remember seeing frozen bodies lying in the snow. Curt got a stack of letters from home on the 5th of January. He quickly opened the first one and saw that the date was from October. He smiled as he read the news from his wife and two daughters. Suddenly Curt stopped reading and looked blankly at the page. He read the line again and again. He couldn't believe what the letter said. He got up and ran to find Andy.

"Andy!" Curt yelled. "Where are you?"

"I'm over here by the fire," Andy answered. Curt ran over and handed Andy the letter.

"Read this, NOW!" he said. Andy poured over the letter slowly and started grinning. He stopped at the same place in the letter.

"Curt, you're having another kid," he laughed. "Congratulations!" It finally hit Curt. He was having another child. He had never felt an emotion like this. Curt missed Myrtle and the girls so much. He felt so happy with the news, yet worried about the future of his young family. Curt quickly sat down and poured out his feelings in a letter.

My sweet Myrtle,
I just got your letter telling me about the baby. I can't believe it! I'm so happy and worried at the same time. By now, you're probably already getting bigger, (I always love when you get big with our babies). I love you and pray that you, the baby, and the girls are healthy and okay. I'm doing fine. I can't really explain what it's like over here. My feelings are so confused. Half the time, I'm so scared. The other half, I just do the job the best I can. It's right that we're here. America has to finish this job, and I'm proud to do my part, but boy, I can't wait to get home to you. I wonder if we'll have another girl or maybe a boy this time. I'll be happy either way. Well, we're moving out. I hope you get this letter soon. Love you! Give the girls a kiss for me.
Your happy husband,
Curt

Sealing the letter Curt joined his buddies, but he couldn't stop thinking about his family.

He had to get home or this child would never meet its dad. He was overjoyed about hearing about his family. His joy did not last for long, however.

"So how many kids is that for you, Curt?" Andy asked.

"This baby will be my third. My other two girls are named Mary and Betty. How about you? Do you have any kids, Andy?" Curt asked.

"I don't have any kids. I do have a fiancée though. I asked her to marry me just before I left to go to war. I hope I get to see her soon." Andy said.

On January 10, the 9th Armored started to make another push into Belgium. Curt was manning the 50 caliber on the back of a jeep. Sgt. Jackson and Andy were in the front of the jeep. They were following a tank column of 20 Sherman tanks. All of the Allies had been ordered to travel at night to confuse the Germans. They were moving through the mountains at midnight. It was pitch black and only a few of the vehicles had lights. Curt was extremely tired and almost fell asleep on the gun.

Suddenly, something drew Curt's attention to the top of one of the hills to his left. A streak of light was flying high into the air, and then it slowly parachuted closer to the ground. The whole American convoy was lit up. Then artillery guns on top of the mountain opened fire. The tanks tried to get off the road as quickly as they could. The first two tanks erupted in flames. At the rear of the column, the men rallied to set up American artillery as quickly as possible. The flare in the sky slowly burned out on the ground. Curt was shrouded in darkness once again. Lieutenant Collins came running up to Sgt. Jackson.

"I want you and a squad of men to go up to the top of the hill and give us the coordinates of their artillery positions. Go NOW!" he yelled. Another tank exploded sending pieces of glowing hot metal flying into the sky.

"Okay, Curt and Andy, ya'll are coming with me. We need to move now!" Jackson said. They quickly made their way into the forest. The forest around them lit up again as another flare came down from the mountain. As they got closer to the summit, they started to hear German voices. Suddenly, a silhouette of a man appeared at the top of the hill. All three men got down behind trees. The German artillery started to fire on the Americans once again: a perfect opportunity to get rid of the man on the hill. Curt looked around the side of the tree and put the crosshairs on the man's chest. As soon as another artillery gun fired, Curt squeezed the trigger. The man went down without a sound. Once again, they were on the move. At the top of the hill, Jackson motioned for Curt and Andy to stay down. About a hundred yards in front of them was the artillery position. Six 88 millimeter cannons and a group of ten mortars were set up. Sgt. Jackson pulled out a map and got on the radio.

"Lieutenant, the gun positions are at 28 degrees North and 72 degrees West. Fire for effect," Jackson said. Ten seconds later, cannon fire from the valley echoed on top of the mountain. It looked like fire was raining down on the Germans. Four of the 88's were immediately blown into pieces along with most of the mortar teams. The remaining Germans ran straight for the tree line. Jackson ordered Curt and Andy to open fire. All three men started unloading on the men coming up the hill, and the Germans never knew what hit them. Every German who was running for the trees was cut down except for one. When he saw that all of his comrades had fallen, he threw down his weapon and raised his hands into the air. He turned around and watched as the rest of the artillery was destroyed.

Sgt. Jackson walked up to him and threw him to the ground beside one of the dead Germans. "Stay on the ground or I will shoot you!" he yelled.

He started yelling in German and holding his hands up. Jackson reloaded his Thompson sub-machine gun and put a bullet in the chamber. He pointed the gun at the poor German's head. Andy started to step forward, but Curt stopped him.

The poor German started crying and yelled in broken English, "Please, I have a family! Mercy!" He then proceeded to rip out a wallet and show the men pictures of his family. The same angry look remained on Jackson's face.

"You don't know what mercy is, *kraut*," Jackson said. He sidestepped the German and started walking down the mountain. Andy and Curt each grabbed one of the prisoner's arms and walked him down the hill. Even from this position, Curt could see multiple burning tanks in the valley below. When they got to the bottom of the mountain, the rest of the men looked like they had been through the wringer. That night, Curt was assigned to protect the German POW because there were a lot of angry soldiers who would have enjoyed shooting the German. Each day, Curt wished more and more that the war would be over soon. He was growing tired of close calls.

CHAPTER NINE

A Case of Mistaken Identity

The start of 1945 was hectic. The whole Allied army was coming together in Belgium to force the Germans out. In January, Curt's division cleared a total of ten towns. After the German counterattack in the Battle of Bastogne, the Germans had lost heart. The only thing that stood in the way of the Allies was the Rhine River. The river was the lifeblood of Germany, and they would defend it to the death.

The worst incident happened in Dirlinburg. When the 9th Armored found the town, no one knew it had existed. The navigators couldn't find it on the map and Allied commanders had no idea where it was. On a cold morning in January, the 9th Armored moved slowly toward the edge of town where it looked like nothing was happening. Curt's jeep edged closer to the entrance of the city. Everyone then slowly moved into the city. Not a shot was fired as they entered the town which had been abandoned by the Germans. Curt breathed a sigh of relief, but it was cut short.

Suddenly Curt heard the unmistakable sound of an artillery attack. Instinctively, he jumped out of the jeep and dove for cover. The shells poured into the city. Fire, dust, and shrapnel flew into the air. The sound was deafening, and everyone was running for cover. Curt tried to move to the nearest house. A shell exploded near Curt, and he was catapulted into the air. He slammed into a door. For a few moments, all Curt could see was black. Then, he felt himself being dragged along the ground. He looked up and saw Andy pulling him into the safety of the house. Inside, Sgt Jackson and Lieutenant Collins were talking. When Curt got inside the house, he slowly got to his feet.

Sgt. Jackson then addressed Andy and Curt. "Boys," he said, "we got to go take out some more German guns."

"Yes, sir!" Curt and Andy said in unison. Suddenly, the shelling stopped.

"This is our chance," Jackson said, "move, move, move!" Curt quickly ran outside into the street, but the carnage stopped him for a moment. A few of the tankers were unable to get out of their tanks in time for the artillery attack. One tank took a direct hit from a shell. One man's leg was gone, and two others were slowly bleeding to death. For a moment, Curt took it all in, but then the sergeant's voice startled him.

"Shirley! Get moving!" Jackson shouted.

He quickly turned and caught up with Jackson and Andy. They ran out of the entrance to the town and quickly headed for the woods. Once again, the artillery started to fire. From the sound of the guns, Jackson thought that they were south of town.

Sgt. Jackson kept the men sprinting to the south until the guns sounded like they were just ahead of them. They slowed down and slowly crept up on the cannons. The guns were still not visible, but they were close. Then the guns became visible, and Curt froze. In the snow, there were ten cannons firing in the direction of Dirlinburg. The guns were being manned by Americans of the 7th Armored.

"STOP! What are you guys thinking?" Jackson yelled at the men. It startled most of the men and they stopped firing.

"Why?" said a Lieutenant, "We have our orders. We're firing at Dirlinburg trying to soften up the Germans."

"The 9th Armored is in Dirlinburg! There are no Germans there!" Jackson screamed.

The enormity of the situation then fell on the Lieutenant. He turned white as a sheet and stammered, "So you mean we have been shooting at our own men."

"Yes, and some have already died," Jackson growled. All the men who were handling the artillery were shocked. They said that they had just gotten orders that morning to fire at the town. After Sergeant Jackson calmed down, the Lieutenant gave Curt, Andy, and Sgt. Jackson a ride back into Dirlinburg. The 9th Armored was in a mess back in the town. In the artillery attack, two tanks had been destroyed, two men had been killed, and twenty injured—by their own forces!

The Lieutenant of the 7th Armored went to talk with

Lieutenant Collins. He tried to explain what had happened and why they had fired on the town, but Collins was furious. "Two of my men are dead!" he screamed. "What am I going to tell their families?"

"We had no idea that you were here. It shouldn't have happened like this," he said.

Two men had died that day for no good reason. After a heated argument, the other Lieutenant finally left Collins alone. After that day, Lieutenant Collins was very wary of entering towns without informing the commanders.

For the rest of January and starting into February, the troops fought toward the Rhine River. No one knew exactly when they were going to get there, but every day they got closer. As they did, Curt tried to take stock of everything that had happened in this war. They had fought through France and lost only a few men. Belgium, however, was a much different story. The German counterattack had scared everyone to death. If the conditions had been different, the Germans could have broken through their lines and killed everyone. Joe died in Bastogne. Curt remembered how after Joe died, he panicked and did things that he normally wouldn't do. He had had no mercy on the Germans, because he had received none from them.

Curt finally figured out what was wrong. He was afraid of dying. He knew the Lord, but he just did not want to die in Europe. He wanted to die in his home when he was old. What would his family do if he died? That was what bothered him the most about dying. He could not think about them suffering.

He finally came to a conclusion about death. He would do anything he could not to die in Europe, but he could accept it if it was meant to be. But he would not accept his friend's deaths. No more of Curt's friends would die under his watch. He would much rather kill than be killed. He prepared himself for the battles yet to come. This war was far from over.

CHAPTER TEN
A Soft Whisper

The bridge was still standing! Ludendorff Bridge had not been knocked down. Curt watched as a group of German tanks moved across the span of the bridge. The commanders of the 9th Armored looked through their binoculars at the town of Remagen and the Ludendorff Bridge. Everyone had expected that the bridge would be at the bottom of the Rhine by now.

Curt received his orders from Sergeant Jackson, "Okay, men. We are going to take that bridge and hold it against any counterattack. Let's go!"

Immediately the whole division, moved down toward the town of Remagen. Curt was assigned as a foot soldier, and he followed the tanks down the hill. The closer they got to the town, the more sniper fire they faced. A few bullets ricocheted off the tank in front of Curt. He had to keep his head down while moving forward. Except for the snipers, most of the Germans had moved on across the Rhine into Germany. The tanks got rid of most of the snipers, and the rest surrendered.

They kept moving forward block by block in Remagen moving closer to the bridge. Suddenly a civilian ran outside one of the buildings waving his arms in the air and yelling something in German. One soldier walked up to him and listened intently. The soldier's expression suddenly changed. He said something back to the man in German, and then ran to the commanders. They seemed interested and then a Colonel gathered everyone together.

The Colonel yelled, "The Germans are planning to blow the bridge at 10:00. It's time to take the bridge!" Curt looked down at his watch. It was 9:15. The tanks started to move again, and Curt got behind one. They faced no resistance going through the city. After five minutes, the bridge came into view. A train on the other side started to depart, but the Shermans quickly put multiple shells into the locomotive.

Lieutenant Collins and Sergeant Jackson suddenly called the 89th Cavalry together. The Lieutenant ordered, "We're going to be the first ones to cross. Get ready to move." Curt looked around and found Andy standing nearby. The group of fifty men moved slowly to the edge of the bridge.

Jackson stood up and said, "Wait for the tanks to barrage the other side, but once it stops, move as fast as you can to the other side." The tanks turned their turrets towards the other shore, and started to fire. The shells exploded against buildings and houses on the other side. The fire suddenly stopped and Jackson yelled, "GO, GO, GO!"

The whole group got up with a yell and started across the two hundred yard span. Two towers on the other side of the bridge opened up with fire. Four MG 42 machine gunners opened fire from the towers. Three soldiers in front of Curt got hit by the machine guns. Curt started to return fire against the Germans, but didn't even bother to aim. When they were a third of the way across the bridge, an explosion rocked the bridge. Curt fell down because of the shaking of the bridge. He was sure that the bridge was going to topple into the water with him still on it. Looking up, he was amazed to see that the bridge was still holding strong. The machine gun fire immediately started again. The American's fire finally started to have an effect. One group of Germans gave up and retreated into town. Curt got up and sprinted as fast as he could toward the two towers. Bullets ricocheted off the floor of the bridge.

Finally, the 89th got across to the other side or what was left of the bridge. The machine guns could no longer fire down from the top of the towers. The Americans split into two groups, and Andy and Curt went into the left tower. A private with a Thompson opened the door slowly and poked his gun through. Someone yelled in German, and the private fired through the door. The group carefully went through the door with weapons raised. When Curt was inside, it took his eyes a few moments to get accustomed to the darkness. The soldiers went from room to room, killing any Germans that dared to fire back.

They cleared the first floor, but they could still hear a lot of Germans on the next two floors. Running up a set of stairs, Andy slightly cracked the door. They primed three grenades and quickly threw them through the crack. The Germans yelled something, but the explosions quickly silenced them. Curt opened the door and surveyed the damage. All of the Germans were dead in that room. Curt went to a window where an MG 42 was mounted. He threw it out the window and into the river. The rest of that floor was checked but held no resistance. When Curt caught up with the rest of the Americans, they had already started clearing the next floor. The third floor only had one room with a ladder leading to the roof. Curt heard a lot of machine gun fire and anti-aircraft fire coming from above them.

Andy decided to be the first up the ladder. He climbed to the top and started to unlatch the hatch above him. A German above the hatch shot through the hatch at Andy. Andy let go of the ladder and landed flat on his back on the stone floor. Curt, along with the rest of his comrades, immediately shot right back through the hatch. The American squad then returned fire through the hatch. The hatch had over a hundred holes in it after they were done. Curt then turned his attention to Andy. Andy had been shot twice in the stomach and was now lying flat on his back. Curt ran to him and said, "Hang on, Andy. We're going to get a medic. Just hold on! MEDIC!" Curt looked up and realized that the men in this building were the only people that could help. There were no medics.

Andy looked up and in a feeble voice said, "Don't leave me here, Curt."

"No one is going to leave you," Curt answered back firmly.

Andy started to get pale and was mumbling inaudibly. Curt knew that he couldn't let another one of his friends die. Then Andy started to whisper something to Curt who leaned down and listened. Andy softly whispered, "Take me home, Curt. Take me home..." With that, Andy slipped away peacefully. Curt laid him down gently and sat there for a second in shock. He looked down at his bloody hands, and then back up at the hatch. He would have to mourn later; there was something else he had to do first. By that time, one of the soldiers had pried the hatch open and tossed a grenade. The explosion echoed and dust flew into the room. Everyone immediately rushed up the ladder to the roof. At the top, Curt discovered three Germans that had finally surrendered to them. Curt walked up to their machine gun and pushed it off into the water.

They looked over to the right and saw the other group of soldiers take the top of the other tower. Ludendorff Bridge had been taken. Curt looked at his watch. It was 10:05. The engineers must have done their job. The first German bridge had finally been captured by the Allies. Curt felt a great sense of relief, but then he remembered another job that he had to do. He climbed down the ladder and walked over to Andy's body. He picked his body up and carried it outside. For a moment the battle was over, but everyone knew that the battle for the bridge had only just begun.

CHAPTER ELEVEN
Dazzling Skies

Ludendoorf Bridge was taken, and all was quiet for the rest of the day. The Germans were either gone or waiting. Curt hoped that it was not the latter. The rest of the day, Curt helped the other soldiers remove the bodies out of the tower that they had cleared. He left Andy's body at last. It was the only American body in the building. Sadly, the bridge was littered with Curt's fallen comrades. Eleven men had lost their lives on the bridge, and five were seriously wounded. So much death and destruction was starting to take a toll on Curt.

That night, Curt stayed in the tower on the bridge. He was one of the first Americans to sleep in Germany during the war. The peace of that knowledge did not last long, however. The next morning Curt was awoken by screaming. When Curt opened his eyes, Sergeant Jackson was standing over him.

"German counterattack," he said coldly.

"What...?" Curt tried to reply but was interrupted by an explosion. He immediately jumped to his feet. He went upstairs to the ladder. He looked up and saw a black object streak by in the gray sky. He climbed the ladder and stood up on the roof. Looking over his shoulder, he saw two dark dots on the horizon. They got closer and closer until they took the form of planes. Sgt. Jackson stepped up to the German anti-aircraft gun mounted on top of the roof. Jackson turned the gun slowly in the direction of the planes and let loose. The four barrels of the gun lit up, and Curt watched as tracers streaked towards the planes. Both planes maneuvered in different directions. They split up and Jackson had to pick one to shoot at. The plane on the right streaked by, and Curt recognized it as a Ju-87 Stuka dive bomber. Curt watched the plane fly over Remagen and drop its bomb. One second later, a plume of fire flew into the air. Jackson was still firing at the other Stuka. He finally got a hit on the plane. Thick black smoke followed the plane as it spiraled out of control toward the bridge. Curt stared in horror. The plane's wing barely missed the bridge as it hurtled into the river.

Curt looked over to the other tower and saw that another soldier had taken his place on the other anti-aircraft gun. The other Stuka, after a successful bombing, flew off toward the horizon.

"Do we have any air cover?" Curt yelled at Sgt. Jackson.

"It will take a little while for them to get here. We have to hold them off until then," Jackson answered. Curt scanned the horizon for any more planes. He felt helpless against the Germans. He had no way to protect himself from their planes. Suddenly, a few more dots appeared on the horizon. The guns turned in the direction of the planes and waited. As they got closer, Curt saw there were not only three Stukas this time, but also two Me-109 fighters. The anti-aircraft guns opened up soon after. Tracers covered the sky. This time around, American tanks, jeeps, and half-tracks also started firing in the direction of the planes. A wall of bullets hurtled towards the planes. One Stuka took a few rounds in the nose, and the engine caught on fire. Suddenly, the fuel tank ignited, and the plane exploded in mid-air. One of the other Stukas was hit in the tail, but remained flying.

The faster more maneuverable Me-109s were getting too close. Sgt. Jackson turned his fire toward them. One of the planes turned toward the towers and started to fire. Curt didn't have much time to move before the machine gun bullets started hitting around him. He dove for the cover of a wall and hunkered down. The machine gun bullets pounded into the tower, blowing out fist-sized holes. The plane flew by overhead, and Jackson finally got a good shot. He shot a few times into the fuselage, and the plane lost control. It veered down and went straight into the river. Curt's counterparts in the other tower managed to shoot down the other Me-109. Then they set their sights on the incoming Stukas.

The dive bombers had circled around and were

coming down the other side of the river. Everyone on both sides of the river was shooting at the two planes. The Stuka with a broken tail was hit again, and the tail fell away from the plane. The plane started spiraling toward the bridge, flew beneath it and hit one of the supports. The whole bridge shook as the support gave way. Amazingly, the bridge remained standing. The other Stuka had gotten into bombing range and dropped its load. Two bombs fell from the plane and hit the bridge. It hit the far side, and the explosion ripped away some of the steel. The plane flew away in victory, only to be ripped apart by 50 caliber bullets. The bridge had sustained some damage, but it was still usable. The Allies needed this bridge desperately to get a foothold in Germany. It couldn't take too many more hits.

"Where is our air cover?" Curt yelled.

"If they don't come soon, there won't be a bridge left to protect," Jackson replied.

A couple minutes later, Curt heard a low buzzing behind him. He turned toward Germany and saw the sky full of planes. The Germans had sent over twenty heavy bombers to finish off the bridge. All the guns on the ground opened up trying to make the planes turn around. As the planes got closer, Curt couldn't escape the impending doom. When those planes opened the bomb bay doors, he was going to die. He looked up at the sky and watched Jackson's attempt to bring down the planes. Suddenly, the front plane was riddled with bullets and erupted in flames. Planes started streaking in from the other side of the river. American P-51 Mustangs flew into the fight.

Curt smiled as the fast fighters attacked the German bombers. The bombers had no chance. They tried to turn around and retreat, but the Mustangs cut into them. Bomber after bomber came hurtling out of the sky. Soon only one bomber was left. It made a desperate attempt for the bridge. It was hit with machine gun fire as the pilot tried to fly into the bridge. He narrowly missed it and crashed on the river bank next to it. Its payload exploded sending fire and shrapnel hundreds of feet in the air.

Curt looked up in the sky, watching the Mustangs circle overhead. That was the most awesome show of force he had ever seen. The sky had blazed with fire and tracers. It was strangely beautiful but also terrible. The job was done for the day, and the bridge was still standing. Curt could tell the Germans were desperate, and they would do anything to win.... anything.

CHAPTER TWELVE
Rain on the Rooftop

The Ludendoorf Bridge stood for a total of ten days after Curt's division took it. Each day German planes and artillery took a toll on the bridge. Almost every German plane found its doom in the Rhine River. Americans had also died every day. The Germans could not stop the Americans from getting tons of supplies into Germany. The engineers stayed busy trying to build a pontoon bridge down the river. They finished it just in time. On the morning of the tenth day, a Stuka made it through the anti-aircraft barrage and dropped a two hundred pound bomb on the center span. At first, the bridge didn't move, but suddenly it started shuddering. A few moments later the center span crumbled and toppled into the water. Then both sides shuttered and toppled in with a giant splash. After a minute or so, there was no sign of the bridge ever being there. The bridge had served its purpose, but now the pontoon bridge was taking most of the load.

The 9th Armored had made the first American stronghold in Germany. The Germans were starting to lose hope. The next day the division got their orders to move deeper into Germany. First, they were going to meet up with the 4th Armored fifty miles downstream. The tanks took the lead as they traveled down the road to the south. After two hours, Curt started to hear gunshots and explosions a couple miles ahead. They quickened their pace and pretty soon another bridge loomed into view. Another bridge to try to capture and hold!

As Curt got closer, he saw a group of Tiger and Panzer tanks firing across the bridge. The Shermans and mobile artillery moved up to the front of the column. Without warning, they opened fire on the Germans. Shell after shell ripped into the tanks. Plumes of fire rocketed out of the German tanks. Four Germans were thrown out of one of the tanks. Curt looked closer and saw that all of them were on fire. They were flailing on the ground in desperation, until one of the Shermans mowed them down with its machine gun. The only tanks that had survived the attack were a few Tigers. The Sherman's shells literally bounced off the heavy armor. The Tigers turned their turrets toward the tanks and opened fire with their 88 mm cannons. Two Shermans in the front of the column exploded and flipped over on their backs. But the giant cannons of the mobile artillery finally silenced the German Tigers.

After the tank battle was over, tanks from the 4th Armored started coming across the bridge. The two armored divisions had a warm meeting and decided to stay in the town for the night. They ended up staying for much more than a day. The next day, the Germans started a counterattack against the bridge. It was all the two divisions could do to hold the bridge against the massive attack. Curt stayed behind his jeep picking off any Germans who took their chances on the open road. For days, the Germans tried to push the Americans back across the bridge. They only came close to succeeding once. They came down the road with a whole division of troops and tanks. Their continuous gunfire kept Curt down behind his jeep. They were getting closer and closer to the bridge, and the Americans were about to sound the retreat. Suddenly, allied air cover arrived. Bombers and fighters filled the skies, and strafed the Germans on the ground. They didn't have any time to escape. The Americans took over a hundred prisoners that day.

The days after that were miserable. The weather had just turned warm enough to melt the snow. A cold rain fell on Curt for three days. The rain soaked through the soldiers' clothes and chilled everyone to the bone. On a miserable February day, Curt and a few other guys were taking a nap in a building near the bridge. The sound of the rain on the rooftop was loud and annoying. What they did not know was that a large group of Germans were using the cover of the rain to move closer to the town. Curt was lying down with his head on the wall, when he felt a vibration come through the house. He sat up slowly and looked outside. Suddenly, an artillery shell landed a couple feet out of the doorway. The concussion of the explosion knocked Curt to the ground. He got up as other shells pounded into buildings around him. Curt thought that he was in relative safety inside the house. Then a section of the roof came down in front of him. After a few minutes the barrage stopped—and the attack began.

The American tanks found defensive positions on both sides of the road. They sat there waiting for the Germans to round the bend in the road. Curt suddenly heard German voices overhead. A pair of Germans with Panzershreck rocket launchers had gotten upstairs somehow. Curt quietly ascended the stairs and opened the door behind them.

"FREEZE!" he screamed at the Germans. The bewildered Germans turned around, and one foolishly raised his Panzershreck to his shoulder. Curt shot the man in the chest, and the German fell through the open window. The other German quickly put up his hands and threw down his weapon. At the same time German tanks moved around the bend in the road. American tanks opened fire and destroyed the enemy tanks. After an hour, the battle stopped raging. For the first time in days, there was peace and quiet.

The next day the Germans did not attack. The

Germans had finally given up on that bridge. After fighting ceased, the clean up duties started. Broken tanks and machinery had to be moved. The bodies had to be buried right away. Soon white crosses filled the fields around the town.

Curt knew he was lucky to be alive after all of the fierce fighting he had endured. In those few days of peace, Curt had a weird foreboding that he would not make it through the war. After a while, the feeling got worse. As always, he prayed that if it was God's will that he would make it home alive from the war to be with his family. But he was less and less sure it would turn out that way.

CHAPTER THIRTEEN
A Dying Eye

The German border on the Rhine River was now secure. For almost two months, the Germans had fought to regain the border. Every one of their counterattacks had failed, and they had finally stopped sending their young men to die. That is not to say that the Americans were doing great. Death hovered over both sides. Open fields around farms were turned into giant cemeteries. Curt had become almost numb to the death he had seen on both sides. He didn't know how many of his friends had died, and he didn't know how many Germans he had killed. He hadn't gotten any mail from home but was pretty sure Myrtle would have had the baby by now. He wondered if he had another daughter or a son.

The good news was that the weather was improving each day. Pretty soon, a nice spring would be upon Europe. Curt finally got to rest after the second battle at the 4th Armored division bridge. On March 28, the division started to move again to the groaning and moaning of the troops. Curt found out that Germany was actually a beautiful country. The snowcapped mountains against the green forests looked like a postcard. Of course the cities looked much different. The Army Air Corps had been decimating the bigger German cities for almost three years now. Not much was left of the buildings.

The first group of German civilians they saw was about a hundred miles into the country. The convoy of tanks and trucks pulled over a ridge, and Curt saw a group of women working in one of the crop fields. They looked up at the Americans and ran away towards the town. Curt thought nothing of it until he heard yelling coming from the town. The American convoy slowed down in anticipation.

"I bet you twenty bucks that there aren't any *Jerrys* in this town," said Dave, a soldier Curt had become closer to since the deaths of Andy and Joe.

"I stopped betting on that kind of stuff a long time ago," said Curt.

Entering a town always left the soldiers the most vulnerable to attack. Suddenly, a Panzer pulled out of the entrance of the town. Immediately, the Shermans opened fire and destroyed it. The convoy moved toward the town and encircled it. Everyone hoped that the Germans would surrender to this show of force. Curt was standing with the 50 caliber waiting for any movement. Suddenly a bullet ricocheted off the side of the jeep. That was enough for Curt. He began to fire away. He shot into all the house windows on his side of the street. Curt saw a rifle come out of a window, and he blew that part of the house away. The Shermans started to shoot into the house, and the Germans could do nothing.

The Mortar teams were getting set up when someone put a white flag on one of the roofs. The soldiers cautiously approached with weapons raised. Curt breathed a sigh of relief when he saw the Germans had thrown down their weapons. They took almost two hundred prisoners from that town. Finally, a town had been won without a fight. The faces of the German prisoners told it all. They were malnourished, sullen, and depressed. The soldiers had lost all hope that they would win the war. Curt thought that Adolf Hitler himself probably didn't think that they could win the war. It was almost pathetic to see them give up this quickly.

A few of the 9th Armored soldiers were assigned to the POW's, and the rest continued forward. On April 1, they took another town in Germany with less resistance than the first. The guys were starting to get cocky because they were not fighting well-trained German soldiers. Some of the German fighters were old men or children. The American soldiers usually had a bed to sleep on every night and were awaiting the formal German surrender. Days passed with almost no combat as they kept traveling farther and farther into Germany. That all changed on April 18.

On the dawn of the eighteenth, everything looked as

normal as it had been in the last few days. Once again, Curt was near the front in his jeep driving through a deep valley full of thick woods. The foreboding of death had ceased in the last couple of weeks, and Curt was looking forward to the day when he would get to see his family again. He thought of Andy and Joe and wished they could have been there for the end of the war. The moment he glanced up, the tree to the left of him burst in half. The top half fell on the Sherman behind him.

"Artillery!" someone yelled. Suddenly 88 mm and mortar shells rained down on the convoy. A thick cloud of smoke and haze covered the air. A tank next to Curt was hit and the explosion sent showers of red hot metal down on him. Curt let out a loud yell and threw himself on the ground. He brushed himself off, but shells were bursting on the ground all around him. Another soldier who was running for cover was hit with a shell. There was nothing left where he was standing. After a few moments the barrage was lifted. The mountains surrounding the valley were lined with German 88 mm cannons. American commanders radioed in for air cover, but it couldn't be there for a few minutes.

Suddenly, German soldiers appeared in the woods. Curt got down on his stomach as the Germans started their attack. He aimed through the scope of his Springfield and shot one German who was carrying an MG 42 to the front lines. He aimed again and shot another who was taking aim at him. By then, the Germans had found Curt's location and started firing at it. He looked back and remembered the 50 caliber on the jeep. When there was a small break in the fighting, Curt dove back toward the jeep and got on the machine gun. He looked down the sight and let loose. The powerful bullets of the gun ripped through the forest and found their targets. The gun did a lot of damage to whoever was on the wrong side of it. He kept firing till he was sure that the Germans on his side of the road were either dead or retreating.

"That's right, *Jerry*. You get out of here," Curt yelled.

He looked back at the convoy and saw all of the other soldiers fighting and the Germans retreating. The Americans were gaining control.

Curt looked back and saw a German plane flying over the road. It was too late, and the Stuka was already too close. Curt aimed the machine gun as fast as he could. Two bombs on the wings dropped off as the plane passed. Curt squeezed off a couple of shots as the plane flew low overhead. One of the bombs hit on the road in the woods, but the other hit its mark. The bomb hit the jeep on the hood and detonated. It flew backwards, and Curt was thrown away from the burning jeep. He hit the ground with a loud thud. When he hit the ground, he noticed a sharp stinging sensation in his neck. Then he looked at the ground beside him and noticed a growing pool of blood. He felt his neck and his fingers touched a piece of metal lodged in his neck. He felt light-headed, but the pain was going away. He reached in his pocket and pulled out a picture. In the picture, it showed Curt smiling with Myrtle and his two girls, Mary and Betty. *But there would be three children now,* he thought. *Soon I will be in a better place.* Strength was leaving his body, and the chaos going on around him seemed farther away and quieter. He felt a strange sense of peace lying there. Darkness closed around Curt, and then he was gone...

CHAPTER FOURTEEN
A Different World

Myrtle reached up to dry her eyes. Mary, Betty, and Jean also had tears running down their faces. The last time any one of them had seen their father was in 1944. Myrtle remembered when she heard the news of his death, and the sadness and loneliness that followed. It is said that time heals all wounds. But it wasn't all that easy. A lot had changed since Curt's death, not only in his family's life but also in the world. She remembered …

The day was May 8, 1945, and America was a happy place because of the Victory in Europe (V.E.) day. Every radio station was covering the story of the unconditional surrender of Germany. When Myrtle heard the news, she literally jumped for joy. She walked into the girls' rooms and said, "The war in Europe is over!"

Mary looked up and said, "Does that mean Daddy is coming home?"

Myrtle smiled and replied, "Yep…" She was interrupted by Mary and Betty yelling for joy. They both ran into baby Jean's room and proceeded to tell her that her daddy was coming home. Myrtle sat back and smiled. Then she remembered some of her friend's family members who would not be coming home. The Johnson family down the street had lost their dad just a few months ago. It looked like they were having a very bad time. Almost every house had silver or gold stars on the front of the house.

Today everyone was celebrating because of the news. At the church, a lot of people gathered to thank God for the war finally ending. Others came to ask Him to help them with their grief. That night Myrtle went to sleep in a joyous mood. She was making plans to see her husband soon for the first time in more than a year.

Myrtle woke to another happy day. She was making a list of things to do to the house to welcome Curt back. That's when she noticed a car pulling up the farm's gravel driveway. She suspected that it was one of her friends coming to talk about the end of the war. She noticed that the car was olive-drab colored. Her eyes widened and followed the car as it moved up the driveway. As it came to a stop, she could clearly see the bright white star on the side of the car. She wasn't prepared for what happened next. Two men stepped out of the car. One of them had an envelope in his hand.

As she looked out the window, a cup slipped out of her hand and crashed to the floor. She couldn't believe her eyes. The two men stepped to the door and knocked on it. She knew what it meant and she couldn't make her feet move toward the door; she didn't want to talk to those men. They knocked again, and finally she slowly walked to the door. She opened it slowly and quietly asked, "Yes?"

A man in a green army uniform spoke up, "Are you Mrs. Shirley?"

"Yes," she answered as tears welled up in her eyes.

"I'm sorry to inform you that Pvt. Shirley was killed in action on April 18. He fought honorably to defend this country, and you have the sympathy of a grateful nation," he said stoically.

For a moment she stood there in silence looking blankly into the sky. She slowly drifted to her knees and started sobbing. One of the men put his hand on her shoulder and let her cry. She cried until she had no more tears left. She found herself questioning why God would take her husband away from her. After she finished crying, she remembered about the children. They would have to know soon what happened to their father. She dreaded telling them more than anything. In the midst of asking God why and how this could have happened, she prayed for the words to give her daughters. Soon they woke from their naps with bright smiles on their faces.

"Momma, why are you crying?" Mary asked quietly.

"I have something to tell both of you," she answered, "Daddy won't be coming home to us." Mary and Betty sat there for a few moments letting everything sink in.

"Is Daddy with God?" Mary asked. For the first time

all day, Myrtle smiled. It took a little girl to explain that Curt was in a better place.

"Yes, honey, Daddy's in heaven with God." She smiled.

That was the beginning of the hard times. Although, their family and friends helped out with everything they could, Myrtle and the girls soon had to find a new place to live. Myrtle decided to rent a place in the mountains on the other side of Clayton. She spent a lot of time on her knees talking with God and trying to figure everything out. It helped when she received that final letter from Curt telling her how happy he was about the baby. Oh, how she wished he could have seen beautiful little Jean! Sometimes the loneliness and worry about taking care of her family was overwhelming. She was learning, however, that God was with her and would always provide for their needs.

A year later, the family was in much better spirits and was starting to heal. One cold night, Myrtle was sitting by the fire when she heard something outside. It was moving against the side of the house. She got out of her chair and went to the closet. She picked up the shotgun and put a shell in the chamber. Myrtle Shirley, although a petite little woman, was like a mother grizzly when it came to protecting her girls. Suddenly, the door knob turned, and the door opened. A tall man walked through the door and was met with the barrel of the shotgun.

"What are you doing in my house?" Myrtle growled.

The frightened man held up his hands and said, "I'm Marcus Caudell. My sister owns this house. I'm sorry. I didn't know anybody was staying here."

Myrtle looked at him and saw something familiar. She asked, "Have I met you before?"

He looked closely at her and said, "Are you Curt's wife?"

"Yes. You do know that he died in the war don't you?" she replied.

"Yeah, I heard as soon as I got back from the Pacific," he replied. She put the shotgun down, and they started to talk. Little did she know that she would later marry Marcus, who had been a high school friend of Curt's. They eventually had four more kids and lived happily for years afterward. Marcus became a father to Mary, Betty, and Jean and loved them like his own. In 1977 he died after a long happy marriage.

EPILOGUE
Finding Closure

MARGRATEN, THE NETHERLANDS, 1987

The contrast of the green grass and the stark white of the markers was absolutely amazing. Thousands of white markers stood in a giant green field on the outskirts of Margraten, Netherlands. They marked the burial site of thousands of heroes from a different era. A group of people surrounded one of these headstones. Each member of the group was dealing with his or her own memories, but one elderly woman had more memories than anyone else. So much time had passed, but she could remember 1945 as if it were yesterday.

This trip had begun as idle talk at one of the family gatherings. Myrtle said it would never happen. But six months later on a warm spring afternoon, Myrtle, three of her daughters, three of her grandchildren and other family members were on a plane to Holland. Myrtle, or Nanny as everyone called her, was a little nervous about this trip. Her husband, Ralph Curtis Shirley, had been buried in this cemetery at the end of World War II. She had never seen his grave. At least she had family members to help her deal with her grief.

After a fourteen-hour ride, the plane finally touched

down in Holland. It was a new and strange place for Myrtle and her family from the northern hills of Georgia. No one spoke English here. The towns were different: some had new, clean-looking buildings, and others looked like they came out of an old black and white movie.

The family rented a vehicle to drive the group to the cemetery which was over three hours away. The countryside was beautiful with its green grass and huge farms. Myrtle tried to imagine what it had looked like when Curt had passed through Holland. They arrived at Margraten and, as the family parked at the front, they were shocked by the size of the cemetery. White headstones stretched for what looked like miles in all directions in front of them. Myrtle pulled a sheet of paper out of her pocket and looked at it intently.

"Curt's grave is in Plot P in Row 19 at Grave 16." Myrtle said. The group made their way past the first plot looking all around at the graves. Myrtle was amazed at how many brave men had died for their country in Europe. She couldn't begin to count the multitude of white crosses that were standing in the fields. A few people here and there were standing by graves honoring their loved ones. As they passed through each plot, Myrtle became more anxious about seeing her husband's grave. She could tell that her three daughters: Mary, Betty, and Jean, were anxious as well.

"Okay, now we are coming up on Plot P," said

Myrtle's oldest daughter Mary. They walked slowly and carefully through the graves. Each daughter carried a large bouquet of flowers to place on the grave. As they got closer to their destination, the emotions of the group began to show. Myrtle reached the grave first, and stood directly in front of it. They formed a circle around the grave.

Carved into the glinting white cross were the words: "Ralph Curtis Shirley. Died Wednesday April 18, 1945 in the service of the United States of America." Each person there read the gravestone and reflected on it. It was a simple grave just like all the others, but it symbolized something important. This man gave his life for the United States. He gave his life to keep his family safe at home and for the future generations who would live after him. He fought to keep America safe and free.

Each person was there to honor his sacrifice and theirs. His wife Myrtle was there to honor the husband that she loved and who had loved her and given her three beautiful daughters. His daughters Mary and Betty were there to honor the father who went off to war to protect them while they were playing at home. His daughter Jean was there to honor the father who she never got to meet and the cause for which he died. Diane, Jackie, and Joanne, three of his grandchildren, were there to honor the grandfather they never knew.

Even though Curt had died at a young age, he had meant so much to so many people. Some of these people he had never even met. The amazing thing they realized is that every grave they passed before they got to Curt's would have had a similar story. Each man in that cemetery had given his life to keep America safe and free.

Myrtle was the first to shed a tear. It was only a single tear that rolled slowly down her face, but it set off the emotions of the other women in the group. For some reason Myrtle actually felt good to be here. It was closure for her to finally see Curt's grave. The group sat there looking at the grave for what seemed an eternity. No one said a word. They just reflected on how much each of their lives had changed because he didn't come home.

Finally, the silence was broken. Mary said, "Mama, what was Daddy like before he went off to war?"

Myrtle smiled and said, "He loved ya'll and always came in after work and played with ya'll. It didn't matter how tired he was, because he loved you. It really hurt him that he had to leave us to go fight, but he did because he cared about you."

Mary said quietly, "I really wish I could have known him better." Everybody in the group agreed with that. But they couldn't get to know him better until they would join him in heaven.

After a few moments, Curt's daughters' husbands read some scripture and spoke about what a good man their dad had been and how proud he would have been of the job their mother had done raising them. Mary read a poem entitled "My Flag." Then Jean brought out some Georgia dirt they had collected from the farm where Curt had been raised. They sprinkled the dirt over the grave as a way of finally bringing him home.

Myrtle reached into her pocket and pulled out a box. Inside was Curt's Purple Heart medal. She laid it down on the grave and said a quick prayer. She then turned away from the grave and slowly walked away. Her family followed close behind. She couldn't help but feel that Curt was smiling down from Heaven on them.